Rob Drummond

The Majority

Bloomsbury Methuen Drama
An imprint of Bloomsbury Publishing Plc

BLOOMSBURY
LONDON · OXFORD · NEW YORK · NEW DELHI · SYDNEY

Bloomsbury Methuen Drama

An imprint of Bloomsbury Publishing Plc

Imprint previously known as Methuen Drama

50 Bedford Square	1385 Broadway
London	New York
WC1B 3DP	NY 10018
UK	USA

www.bloomsbury.com

**BLOOMSBURY, METHUEN DRAMA and the Diana logo
are trademarks of Bloomsbury Publishing Plc**

First published 2017

© Rob Drummond, 2017

British Library Cataloguing-in-Publication Data
A catalogue record for this book is available from the British Library.

ISBN: PB: 978-1-3500-5905-4
ePDF: 978-1-3500-5907-8
ePub: 978-1-3500-5906-8

Library of Congress Cataloging-in-Publication Data
A catalog record for this book is available from the Library of Congress

Series: Modern Plays

Cover image © David Stewart

Typeset by Mark Heslington Ltd, Scarborough, North Yorkshire
Printed and bound in Great Britain

To find out more about our authors and books visit *www.bloomsbury.com*.
Here you will find extracts, author interviews, details of forthcoming
events and the option to sign up for our *newsletters*.

The Majority

Rob Drummond

Rob   **Rob Drummond**

Director   David Overend
Designer   Jemima Robinson
Lighting Designer   Michael Harpur
Music and Sound   Scott Twynholm
Associate Video Designer   Mogzi Bromley-Morgans

The Majority was first produced at the National Theatre, London on 14 August 2017

Originally co-commissioned by the Arches and NT

The Majority

It is enough that the people know there was an election. The people who cast the votes decide nothing. The people who count the votes decide everything.

– Stalin

To The Arches Theatre Company

Author's Note

It is always a tough task to put down in words the plays in which I perform. Publishers' deadlines dictate that the version of the script you are reading now is the version that existed going into rehearsals. It is complete. It is considered. It works. But it will undoubtedly be very different to the play that audiences will see.

We simply don't know, until we try this material out in front of our rehearsal audiences, what will remain and what will change. They will have the chance to play with our voting pads and influence the shape and content of the show itself. In past shows entire sections have disappeared, the word count has been decimated and new endings written on the fly. But please don't feel short changed because the version you're reading, believe me, is far from an incomplete, rushed or half-baked version.

I started work on this play three years ago as a reaction to the Scottish independence referendum of 2014 and it has gone through more drafts than any play I have ever worked on, largely because the world kept changing, rendering entire drafts either redundant or dated. I am writing this note now, in the wake of two terrorist attacks in London and one in Manchester, in a world that is not only trying to work out what to do about this growing problem, but also what the nature of the problem even is.

If the writing of a script is a discussion between the author and the world, then rewriting is that author being intellectually honest in their quest to discover the truth of what they are striving to say. Similarly, it seems to me the only way to approach political or social problems is by continually talking in an open, honest and non-precious way, tearing up old ideas that no longer fit and accepting that, in lieu of a perfect solution, there should always be ongoing dialogue, ongoing improvement. Unfortunately we are currently experiencing a crisis in dialogue and the death of nuance, as far right and far left voices scream across the void at each other in a kind of vitriol vs virtue signal battle for the ages. It's happening as I write, with this latest attack bringing out the worst in both sides – this either has *nothing to do with Islam* or *all Muslims are terrorists* – without much sensible discussion in between.

This play is about ideas. How do we communicate our ideas effectively? How do we best decide what is right? And what happens when 49 per cent of us disagree?

Rob Drummond

Director's Note

Working on *The Majority* has made me think more theatrically about politics, and more politically about theatre.

The language of the stage is routinely used to dismiss and deride the world of politics: we bemoan the *staged-managed* appearances of politicians; and the *dramas* and *performances* that are *scripted* for them *behind the scenes*. There is an inherent distrust of theatre in this rhetoric; a suspicion of the fictitious, rehearsed and spectacular.

But might theatre be granted a more positive and progressive role in political debate? The stories we tell, and the way we tell them, can help us to better understand ourselves, and the world we live in. It seems that we need this now more than ever. While a performance may not have a direct impact on real-world events, theatre is a space to test and interrogate our ideas and opinions, to empathise with people in difficult situations and, importantly, to gather together in the shared moment of an encounter.

The theatre audience might be usefully thought of as a microcosm of a wider political community. While they may loosely share certain characteristics and world-views, they are a group of autonomous individuals who have invested in something and agreed to come together to try to make it work. This temporary coalescence of otherwise unrelated people is a powerful thing. It doesn't mean we have to think the same, or stay together after the event, but in the time and space of the performance, we share an experience and, hopefully, we leave having learnt something about each other.

While *The Majority* is, of course, a show about political majorities, it is also about the power and potential of the theatre audience. It asks us to form a collective, but also to be aware of those close to us who may feel differently. It is about the need to argue better, engage in difficult conversations and avoid the impulse to lash out. The theatre is offered as a place to play with these relationships and dynamics, and to perform the role of a political community, with all the agency and responsibility that entails.

This play is structured around a series of increasingly challenging dilemmas: mini-referenda on narrative, ethics and morality. These votes won't have an immediate effect – they won't elect new leaders or change constitutions – but they will have been considered and cast, and they will affect the performance. The audience always has an active, critical role to play in shaping meaning and creating drama, but the voting sections of *The Majority* make that role explicit, and explore the relationship between the individual performer and the crowd of spectators.

Rob Drummond is on his own out there, on an empty stage surrounded by the audience on all sides. This is at once an extremely powerful and terrifyingly vulnerable position for a performer to be in. Early in the performance, Rob asks the audience to vote on the latecomer policy for the evening. Clearly, he sets the terms for this decision, but this moment is also a symbolic handing-over of control to the will of the majority. Rob genuinely appeals to the audience throughout the performance, testing his individual perspective against the decisions of the majority.

The choices may be limited; and the outcome may be *theatrical*, *illusory* or *staged*; but this is a real community making real decisions, and directly experiencing the impact of these choices. We recognise the theatricality of politics. Perhaps a greater awareness of the power of theatre can, in turn, teach us something about our agency and responsibility in the world outside. We all have a role to play.

David Overend

Act One

This play should be performed by one actor. The audience have voting pads by which they can vote only Yes or No.

A swarm of bees fly around the room as the audience enter.

Scene One

March 2016.

A mugshot image of Rob Drummond appears in the space.

Rob   23 March 2016. I am under caution at Victoria Road Police Station in Aberdeen. My rights have been read, my prints taken and my soul digitally removed by a 2010 Canon power-shot camera.

What I am about to tell you is the truth. More or less. But in deciding which events, quotes and facts to leave in and which to eliminate I am . . . focussing reality for you. For your benefit. You may find yourself thinking, that's too neat to be true. And it will be. I will have moved a pleasing motif, an image, a line, a thought, from one place to another because . . . this is a play after all.

This mugshot for example. It happened. But we couldn't get our hands on the real ones so we mocked them up. For you.

So. How did I, a respectable, mild-mannered, law-abiding individual with no criminal record, end up here?

Scene Two

Present day.

Rob   Hello and welcome to *The Majority*. When you entered the theatre you should have been given electronic voting pads. The first thing we need to do is test these pads out to make sure they work because tonight we will be trying to agree on the fairest possible solution to a series of propositions.

Because more than anything, that's what I'm looking for. Agreement. Concord. An end to the fighting. Okay?

So, I will be setting a number of referenda that we will be voting on as the show progresses and your job is simply to press one for Yes and two for No.

So our first, warm-up, proposition, to test the pads, is simple.

This community understands and accepts the voting system for the show tonight.

That is the proposition. Press one for Yes if you agree with this. And obviously two for No.

The audience vote. **Rob** *comments on the result, shown somewhere in the space.*

Who voted no? You are free to leave the theatre at any time if you're not happy with the community decision.

In fact, that reminds me. Before we properly get started we should vote on something of vital importance.

The latecomer policy.

Some of you won't mind latecomers shuffling into their seats, disrupting the show, making noise and putting the performer off, taking you out of the carefully constructed world he's created. And others, like me, will find it nothing short of unacceptable. You know the start time of the show, I mean, come on. We all managed it.

So. The second proposition I wish to put before you is as follows.

This community wishes to ban all latecomers.

Vote one for Yes and two for No.

The audience vote. **Rob** *comments on the result.*

Rob   We've shut the borders.

(*Or*) We've opened the borders!

The policy is put in place.

Now, before we continue I'd like to get a rough idea of who today's community is. So, if you could please answer Yes or No to the following questions as they relate to you personally.

Rob *asks a series of questions which may include some or all of the following.*

This community is liberal.

This community is male.

This community is white.

This community is pro-choice.

This community believes in the death penalty.

This community believes in God.

This community believes in absolute freedom of speech.

This community believes they can make a difference.

Rob *collates the results in their entirety and creates a profile for the community. Something like . . .*

So. This community is a liberal, white, pro-choice, anti-death penalty, female. This community believes in God but does not believe absolutely in freedom of speech. This community believes they can make a difference.

That is who you are.

The majority has spoken.

Scene Three

September 2014.

Rob   It's 19 September 2014. The day after the day
Scotland voted against its own autonomy. It's the result we
were kind of expecting. But it doesn't hurt any the less.

George Square is a mess of blue and white flags and vodka
and Irn-Bru bottles. The clean-up has begun and all around
sit teary-eyed Scots trying to come to terms with what has
happened as police keep order and offer hugs.

There are 1,617,989 Scots who need hugs this morning. And
2,001,926 cunts, as Frankie Boyle helpfully points out on
Twitter. Isn't that nice?

A car drives by with a 'NO' sticker on the back window. It
stops at a red light. Someone throws a vodka bottle at it. I
slip away.

As I say, I'm looking for agreement, not conflict.

England, I'm told, breathed a sigh of relief at the result.
After all, communities are stronger together. Unless you're
talking about Europe of course.

How many of this community breathed a sigh of relief? Let's
see shall we?

**This community believes the result of the Scottish
independence referendum of 2014 was a good thing for the
rest of the country.**

They vote. **Rob** *comments on the result.*

Selfish fucking bastards.

(*Or*) It's a shame this counts for nothing isn't it?

A drunk comes up to me and puts his arm around me.

Drunk   Sokaypal. We'll getemanexttime!

Rob   And he gives me a big kiss.

He thinks I'm one of them. He thinks I voted Yes.

When the truth is . . .

The truth I've never told a soul in Scotland, before now, is . . .

I didn't vote at all.

Wait. It's worse than that.

I had never voted. Ever.

There. I've said it.

I had thought about it, back when I was first eligible. But politics . . . Watching them shouting at each other on TV. Seeing what it did to families. I mean my mum's a Tory and my dad's a Labour man and they . . . well I grew up to the sound of shouting matches. All that shouting and, really, nothing changes.

So long ago I had decided to retreat. To look after my immediate friends and family. And myself. And that's it. If we can never agree on what's right then what's the fucking point in trying?

So why am I in George Square then?

Well, I'm here because Ben Power, the man with the greatest name in British theatre, had called me up that very morning to ask me if I was interested in writing about the politics of independence for the National Theatre.

Of course, Ben. Yes, Ben. Incredibly important, Ben. Such an important topic. I love politics. We can make a difference, Ben. We can!

It's the National Theatre. Give me a break.

So I've come to George Square for inspiration. And all I've received is a sloppy kiss from a drunken Scot.

The next month I'm down here for a meeting with Ben and he asks me what I want to write about.

I had nothing. Nothing. I was on the verge of telling him the truth, the whole truth. I'm a fraud. A non-human. A self-disenfranchised drop-out. When it came to me.

The worst idea I've ever had.

I want to write about: William Wallace.

Ben   William Wallace?

Rob   Yeah, Ben. I really feel that by going back to the source we can say something important about the present. About what independence means now as opposed to then.

Pulled that one out of my arse.

Ben   Okay. Well. I know someone you should talk to – someone the NT use from time to time on our history plays. If you really do feel passionately about this?

Rob   I do, Ben. I really do.

So off I went to Royal Holloway, University of London to interview a history professor by the name of . . .

Duncan   Greg Duncan. How do you do?

Rob   Professor Duncan is a Scotsman in England. A broken man. There is a peeling 'Yes' poster on the wall behind him. I decide not to mention it but he brings it up on his own.

Duncan   I couldn't vote you know. Lived there all my life. One year down here and I don't get a vote in the most important referendum of my lifetime.

Rob   Anyway, I'm writing about William Wallace and I was wondering . . .

Duncan   Why are you writing about him?

Rob   Well, you think independence you think . . .

Duncan   You do know we know next to nothing about him don't you?

Rob   Nothing?

Duncan   I have a colleague who says he didn't even exist.

Rob   Really?

Duncan   Yeah. We don't speak. He voted No. Of course.

Fucking No voters. How dare they stop Scotland becoming fairer. I mean who votes against fairer? Who votes against autonomy? And why no third option? Eh? One point six million people. Ignored. It makes me fucking sick.

Rob   So there's nothing on Wallace at all?

Duncan   Nothing much. You'll have to make it all up, son.

Rob   I don't want to do that.

Duncan   I take it you voted Yes?

Rob   Yeah. Course I did.

Duncan   Quite right.

Rob   A friend of mine didn't vote at all.

Duncan   Scum. I mean that. Scum. Contemptible. One thing worse than someone who doesn't shout their opinion squarely in the opposition's face and that's someone who doesn't have an opinion to shout. Still could have been worse, you could have tried to sell your vote on eBay. Like that clown up north.

Rob   What did you just say?

And just like that, I have my play. A man who sells his vote on eBay. Fascinating. The morality of it. It's his vote after all. Why shouldn't he be allowed to sell it? I wish I'd thought of it!

Fuck William Wallace.

I rush home and google the shit out of this. Scottish man sells vote on eBay. First hit. Eric Ferguson. From a tiny town up between Thurso and Aberdeen on the north-east coast. The article doesn't tell me much. He wasn't jailed. Verbal warning. It's a comedy article. Makes him seem a bit of a fool. Doesn't even say why he did it.

I wonder if he's on . . . he is. Twitter. And he's quite active. About four or five posts a day.

'Things will never change until we own the means of production.'

'Look out! Crooked Tory councillors don't care about you. Nazi scum.'

'We don't want anything special, just the right to decide our own fate.'

'How the Illuminati is controlling the banks.'

I go back to the time of the referendum.

'A dark fucking day for Scotland. A socialist country run by capitalist scum. And we just voted to keep it that way. I'll be drinking if you need me.'

His handle is Eric@SocialJusticeApiarist (that's a fancy word for a bee keeper) and his chosen picture is him standing in a field covered in bees.

Do I really want to make contact with Social Justice Bee Keeper? He sounds like the world's worst superhero.

I've got nothing else and a deadline looming. So I send him a direct message.

'Dear Eric, I'm writing a play about independence for the National Theatre (England). Would you like to talk to me about selling your vote? I'll be kind. Honest! :)'

I add a hashtag to seal the deal: '#nevervotedtory'.

Hey. It wasn't a lie.

Scene Four

Present day.

Rob *notices that there is something on the screen. It is one of two things.*

Either, a bunch of latecomers who are being told they cannot come in; **Rob** *and the audience watch in silence as they are asked to go, argue with staff and eventually leave. One of them is teary.*

Or, one or more latecomers are allowed into the space.
Congratulatory music is played, welcoming them into the space. It's a real event. A celebration of the fair mindedness of the audience.

(Perhaps **Rob** *welcomes the latecomers and asks them all the questions they have missed, which creates a strange atmosphere as they are less protected by anonymity as* **Rob** *finds out who they are and sees if that tallies with the rest of the audience.)*

Should the policy be to allow latecomers and no latecomers appear, the music still plays but no one comes in. **Rob** *comments on what a waste of time the whole enterprise has been.*

Scene Five

May 2015.

Rob   15 May 2015 and Eric has not replied. But I'm sure I'm onto something and I've begun writing the first draft of 'The Man Who Sold His Vote'. It's about a guy in a semi-futuristic quasi-UK who tries to sell his vote on eBay and is arrested for it and put through the courts as an example to others who might try to disenfranchise themselves in protest to the system. It's basically Russell Brand's wet dream.

It's hard to imagine now but at the time I was really quite excited about it.

I'm round my parents for Sunday dinner and I'm telling them all about it.

I mean, why shouldn't he sell his vote, eh? It's his vote!

My dad's not happy with this.

Dad   My father fought and died so that . . .

Rob   Your dad's still alive! We saw him last week.

Dad   Other people's fathers then! They fought and died so you could vote.

Rob   No. He fought so I could be free to choose whether to vote or not!

My mum's feeling left out. She decides to join in.

Mum   I like voting. Makes me feel like I'm doing my bit. And I always get the answer right.

Rob   What?

Mum   I always get it right. Like independence. I voted No and that was the right answer.

Rob   There's no right answer, Mum.

Mum   Then why do we bother asking people?

Dad   The right answer was Yes. We got it wrong.

Rob   Says my dad eating a chip from a plate with so much salt on it you could write your name in it.

Mum   We asked people what the right thing to do was and they told us. And I got the right answer.

Rob   It's not right just because most people think it.

Mum   Yes it is. That's how it works. We decide what's right, what's moral, by voting on it. Don't we?

Dad   Moral! This coming from a Tory voter.

Rob   The Tories have just won the general election with a bigger majority than anyone expected. And the SNP have yellow washed Scotland. The map of the UK looks famously like Maggie Simpson.

The country has never been more divided.

Mum   All I know is that I voted Conservative and the Conservatives won. Babs does it again.

Rob   So let me get this right, Mum. You think that if a majority of people want something that automatically makes it morally correct?

Mum   Do you have a better way of deciding?

Rob   But people used to think slavery was correct.

Mum   In those days maybe it was.

Rob   What the fuck did you just say, Mum?

Mum   Language!

Rob   Are you really telling me that slavery was once moral?

Tell me this. If Northern Ireland had a vote on gay marriage and the result came back No, would that mean it was immoral to be gay in Northern Ireland?

Dad   The reason they've never had that vote is because they're scared that's exactly what would happen.

Rob   What about abortion. If a majority banned it would that be right?!

Mum   If that's what those people decided. Otherwise what's the point in asking them?

Rob   Fuck. You're a bigot. You're a total bigot.

Mum   Ocht, don't get all worked up. It's not like it's real anyway. It's all just nonsense.

It would just be nice if everyone could agree, wouldn't it?

Rob   Yes. It would.

Mum   As long as what they all agreed with was what you thought already.

Rob   A long silence. I silently fume. My mum keeps stumbling into very good points.

Is morality just what the majority say? Is that all it is? If I don't vote, I'm not part of that discussion.

But the discussion is pointless.

Don't worry about it. She's right. None of it's real. It's all just nonsense.

Deep breath.

Control yourself.

Dad   So have you spoken to this man? This guy who tried to sell his vote?

Rob   He's not replied. I might have to give up on him.

And would you believe it . . .

At this precise moment . . .

Nothing happened. But then later, as I was getting ready for bed . . .

My phone beeped.

Eric had finally replied.

Scene Six

Present day.

Rob   There is a runaway train car heading towards five railway workers. There's no time to warn them. They will die if it hits them. You are standing by a lever which, when pushed, will send the train car onto a siding on which there is a single workman. If you push the lever you will kill him but the five workers will be saved.

What is the correct decision? What is the moral decision?

The proposition is this . . .

This community would push the lever.

Please vote now, Yes or No.

The result comes in and hangs in the air.

I can see some of you are anxious to explain your answer. Unfortunately that's not how this works.

Scene Seven

May–August 2015

Rob   Between May and August of 2015 Eric and I exchange countless messages, beginning with his reply to my initial query.

Eric   Dear sir, I would be interested in speaking with you but am always wary of the motives of anyone who voluntarily reaches out to me. What's your angle?

Rob   Eric. I don't have an angle. The truth is, I'm a little like you. I don't vote. I just keep my head down. But I've got this commission and I need to find something to write about. Selling a vote seemed an interesting story, that's all.

Eric   You've got me all wrong, sir. I do vote. I chose to do this to draw attention to something, but when the media showed up they just took the piss. How do I know you won't do the same?

Rob   I can guarantee I won't disrespect you. And I won't use any material if you explicitly forbid it.

There's a long delay before the next reply. Two weeks in fact. And then . . .

Eric   Fine. What do you want to know?

Rob *sits and 'faces'* **Eric**.

Rob   Why did you do it?

Eric   Because this place is overrun by Nazis.

Rob   Fair to say not the reply I was expecting.

Eric   Our local council is made up of twelve councillors elected from here and three neighbouring towns. Three of our four are Nazis.

Rob   What do you mean Nazis? Like the Nazi Party?

Eric　Nope. Up here it's mainly independents at council level.

Rob　So they are independents?

Eric　Yes.

Rob　So how do you know they're Nazis?

He tells me the councillors in question, and I won't name them because it's not fair, have affiliations with a local group called White Hand. And that organisation does exist because I googled them. But from what I could see they were active nearer Aberdeen, not out where Eric lived.

How do you know they are affiliated with them?

Eric　Because I keep my ear to the ground.

Rob　Hardly convincing.

What have they done so far to make you worry, these councillors?

Eric　Nothing yet. But they're taking a vote on an immigration issue in a month's time. And I bet I know what way they'll vote.

Rob　The immigration issue concerns the proposed resettlement of refugees from Syria. This is around the time that ISIS were really getting a foothold in the country and local councils across the UK were asked to consider taking a hypothetical group of displaced citizens.

So if they vote against it . . .

Eric　Then we'll know for sure.

Rob　Cards on the table, my initial impression of Eric, simply from his words on a computer screen . . . He's a nutbag. A paranoiac.

But he grew on me. Over those first few months of exchanges.

Here's his response, as close as I can remember, to me
mocking the idea of Trump running for office.

Eric   Don't you fucking laugh, it will happen. You'll see.
Trump for president. The world's going that way.

Rob   So, clearly not the fool I maybe first thought.

And he was funny too. This is him talking about his bees.

Eric   I fucking love my bee,s Rob, they keep me in beer!
Honey money, baby! Did you know most bees are solitary,
not communal? Not a lot of people know that. Communal
bees are rare and dying out. They're a real unit you know.
No dissenting voices. Total harmony. But the best thing
about them – if a solitary bee stumbles across them, they
don't attack. They welcome them in. If they want to come in.
And they adopt the fucking bee. Now I think if we could be
more like bees, then we'd be onto something!

Rob   I found out he had a wife, Lucy, and a child, Morag.
They were still together but lived separately, which was odd
but seemed to work for them.

Eric   I need my alone time and fuck knows they need time
away from me.

Rob   And he had a scientific mind, which is something I
could relate to. He didn't believe in God. He believed in
science.

Which is how he trapped me.

Eric   Let me ask you something, sugar tits.

I think he'd had a few beers when he composed this message
but I'm reading it to you as I received it.

You don't vote so you don't care, right?

Rob   No. I do care. I'm just logical about it. It's not negative
to realise we're all fucked, it's sensible. Did you know there's
a galaxy, a whole fucking galaxy headed on a collision course
with ours at the moment. We *know* it's all for nothing.

Okay, I might have had a few too.

Eric   And when does this galaxy hit? Next week?

Rob   All I mean is that nothing I can do, objectively, will do any good to change the way things are going.

Eric   Have you ever tried?

Rob   I suppose not.

Eric   So you've made a conclusion without testing the hypothesis.

Rob   What do you mean?

Eric   You've decided that nothing you do will make a difference but you've never tested that by doing something.

Rob   Alright then. I'll vote in the next election or referendum or whatever.

Eric   I'm not talking about voting. I'm talking about action. Real action. Like I used to do. Back in the eighties.

Rob   What did you do?

Eric   You know I don't talk about that shit online, Rob. Nice try.

Rob   Why don't you?

Eric   Everything I say, on the phone, on here, is monitored by the government. I don't think that, Rob, I know that. All I'll say is, my name wasn't always Eric.

Rob   You changed it?

Eric   Come up and see me. Help me campaign. Test your hypothesis. And I'll tell you all about it.

Pause

Rob   Go up and visit crazy bee man?

Well . . .

It would make for a good second act for my play.

Act Two

Rob *travels north on a train.*

Scene One

September 2015.

Rob As I step off the train in Thurso, which is the northernmost train station on the British mainland, I see a little man with a tweed jacket and a cap pulled down over his eyes sitting on a bench with a sign that reads 'Drummond'. I've arranged a car to take me the rest of the way as there's really no other way of doing it. I approach him only to find he's asleep. I gently place my hand on his shoulder and . . .

Old Man Fuck you!

Rob He swipes at me with the back of his hand, catching me on the chin.

I point at his sign.

Eh. I'm Drummond.

At this point you'd expect at the very least an apology. An explanation. I was in a war. I have PTSD. I've been mugged in my sleep before.

But no. He just nods and walks away. I work out for myself to follow him and he leads me to a twenty-year-old BMW. I get inside. It reeks of dog.

The old man gets in the front. He knows where we're going.

Old Man Why you going there?

Rob I'm meeting with Eric Ferguson.

*The **Old Man** laughs.*

Rob You know him?

Old Man Oh aye, I know him.

Rob   He seems to think there's a Nazi problem up here.

The old man suddenly becomes very serious. And then he says one word, which I'm not sure how to take.

Old Man   Problem?

Rob   I decide to put my headphones in for the rest of the journey. I'd rather not know what this guy thinks about Nazis to be honest. I don't want to risk getting in an argument and being kicked out the car on a country road in nowheresville.

The journey takes us two hours. The town, which I'm not going to mention the name of, is a sleepy little poverty-stricken fishing town. Not exactly where you'd expect to find the base of a burgeoning Nazi resurgence.

Eric's house is modest enough. A semi-detached near the high street with a view of the North Sea. Not bad.

I ring the doorbell and wait for a few minutes but no one appears so I let myself round into the back garden.

And there he is.

Standing at the bottom of a relatively small garden with thousands and thousands of bees buzzing all around him. He's not wearing a bee keeper's helmet. Just a hat. His face is uncovered and so are his arms.

I should make it clear that this garden was way too small for so many bees. And they were buzzing their way towards me now. Almost as if they could sense my fear.

Social Justice Bee Keeper just stood there staring at me.

He's set this up. He knew I was arriving now. He's done this for me.

He shouts over at me, but I can barely hear him over the buzzing.

Eric   ROB!

Rob   ERIC!

Eric   YOU'VE CAUGHT ME UNAWARES!

Rob   Aye, right.

CAN WE GO IN THE HOUSE?

Eric   WHAT?

Rob   I DON'T WANT TO GET STUNG!

As I'm saying this, well, alright it was a few days later but it's better for the story if it's now, as I'm saying this a bee stings me. My first ever bee sting. Which Eric finds hilarious.

CAN WE GO INSIDE?!

Eric   ALRIGHT, YOU BIG JESSIE. THE BACK DOOR'S OPEN.

Rob   I leap at the invitation to get out of the bee garden and into the house. And after a legitimate twenty minutes Eric joins me.

He's around fifty-five years old I guess. A wiry wee guy with a scrawny beard and a face that launched a thousand Rizlas. Yellow teeth through a broad, almost manic smile. Red bee-sting weals all over. Constant movement. Everything's urgent. He seems happy. That's the thing I really remember. Just a happy man. Hope in his eyes.

Not what I was expecting.

He makes me some tea, toast and honey and I accept all despite liking none. And before I can even properly say hello he launches into one of the most astonishing monologues I've ever heard.

I've tried my best, as with most of this, to remember what he said.

It went something like this . . .

Eric   The Nazis. They sell cocaine to the kids. All over the place. People think I'm on cocaine but I'm not. I'm just naturally energetic. If anything I need drugs to slow me down. A little bit of weed to take the edge off my brain you know. We can do some later if you like. Anyway, Rob, let me tell you, I'm on to them. And they know it. And one day they're going to kill me for it. I'm telling you, if I die, they did it! Most fishing towns they have a drug problem because, well, it's fucking boring here. And a few years back this Nazi group moved in down the road and starting selling. Now, you're going to think this is mental, right, but bees, they have better smelling than dogs, right, and they take shorter to train – you just get them to associate the coke with a reward of sugar water and, bang, the next time they smell coke their little proboscises shoot out and you know – fuck, that's cocaine. I'm not joking, there will be sniffer bees at airports within the next ten years. So, I thought, fuck me, I can train my bees to sniff out the coke. So I went to the police and asked them for some coke so I could get started with the training and I told them that if they helped me we could uncover the whole thing and get them all locked up. But they were having none of it. And that's when I realised that they were in on it too. All of them. The police, the council. They're all in on it.

Rob   It's at this point I ask myself what I'm even doing up here. I could have written my play without this visit. Something about Eric though is undeniably intoxicating. I found myself wanting his stories to be true. I mean they obviously weren't. Or at least there was so much untrue about them so as to totally undermine the truthful bits. But still . . . Nazis. We all hate Nazis right? Little disagreement there.

We spent the weekend together. He took me up to the house he called the Nazi compound. Disappointingly no one was home. He said they had many bases all along the coast. It seemed far fetched to me. I mean, why? Why move in up here?

Eric   Why not? It's not like this is the only place they are.
They're all over the UK now. Part of the far-right
resurgence.

Rob   I found myself trespassing that first night. We scaled a
fence and went right into the compound. Looking for
evidence of drugs. And Nazis. A swastika of coke I think
would have sealed the deal . . . but we saw nothing.

On the second night we mainly just hung out down the
seafront eating fish and chips. His wife Lucy and his
daughter Morag join us. I get the sense that Lucy is reticent
to talk about Eric. I'm desperate to know more about why
they live apart but I don't want to ask something so personal
so soon.

Eric later tells me that she has something called dissociative
disorder. A form of depression that means nothing feels real
to her. A kind of defence mechanism against the world he
says. Having a discussion with her is like talking to a stoned
artificial intelligence. She met Eric shortly after he came up
to the community, around fifteen years ago. I ask her about
the Nazis and she says . . .

Lucy   Oh yeah, Nazis, man. Everywhere.

Rob   Morag wants to go so Lucy kisses Eric and says she
loves him and she'll see him tomorrow.

And then they leave. To go to their separate house.

I ask Eric about the local community. What do they all think
about the place?

Eric   There's two types of people. Those who keep their
heads down and those who look for a fight wherever they
can find one. And guess which one's going to make the
difference in the world?

Rob   The second one.

Eric   This place is full of the first type. Like most places.
These days I need to go onto the internet to find an
argument.

Rob   On the third night, Eric offers me some weed. To be honest the weekend has been a little bit dull. He wanted me to come up and 'help him campaign' but I didn't see much campaigning going on at all.

I took the weed.

And I inhaled.

And it was good.

Eric   So, tell me about the play, Rob.

Rob   I don't know, man, I don't know, it's like I see it and then it drifts away. It was going to be about you selling your vote but . . . I don't think there's enough in that.

Eric   You should write about this place. Get our story out there.

Rob   But there isn't much of a story is there, Eric?

He stops short and puts his cigarette down.

Eric   You. Follow me.

Rob   And I did. Out into the back garden where Eric picked up some sort of package and then off out down the main street, high as a kite, looking up at the blanket of stars in the sky and thinking, I don't know where we're going but this is fucking fun!

We arrive in front of a house. Much like any other.

Eric   This is where she lives.

Rob   Who? Lucy?

Eric   No. The councillor.

Rob   Whose name I will not mention.

Eric   She voted against the immigrants coming. Like I knew she would.

Rob   She did?

Eric They all did. All four of them. But the rest voted them down. So it's going to happen.

Rob Good.

Eric No one else round here even cares.

Rob At least they lost.

Eric Put this through her letter box.

Rob What?

Eric Put it through her letter box.

Rob What is it?

Eric It's bees.

Rob I swear he said this like it was the most normal thing in the world.

I'm not putting bees through her letter box.

Eric She's got to know she can't get away with this shit.

Rob We can't do that.

Eric Do you think we should take immigrants?

Rob Well, yes I do but . . .

Eric Then put this through her letter box.

Rob No.

Eric Fine. I will then.

Rob No. Wait.

How did I get here? In a small northern fishing town trying to persuade a mad socialist not to drop bees through a Nazi's letter box.

Let's do something else.

Eric Like what?

Rob We'll write something.

Eric   Like what?

Rob   Here.

And at this point I picked up a big chalky stone from the ground, I got down on my hands and knees and I carved into the ground right outside her house the words . . .

'NAZI SCUM'.

I wasn't sure she was one. In fact, I was pretty certain she was just plain old right wing but, well, fuck her. She voted against helping actually desperate human beings. And I was saving her. From waking up covered in bees. And I was saving myself too. From a potential confrontation. And I was saving Eric, from himself. I was doing the right thing here. For the greater good.

Eric looked down at my handiwork.

She'll see it when she leaves the house tomorrow morning, I say.

Eric   Well. It's a start.

Rob   As we walk away from the house I notice a child's seat in the car on the driveway.

Scene Two

Present day.

Rob   There is a runaway train car heading towards five railway workers. There's no time to warn them. They will die if it hits them. You are standing on a bridge with a large fat man. If you push this man off the bridge his girth would be enough to stop the train car. He would die but the five workers would be saved.

It's the same as before, but you have to push a human, not a lever.

What is the correct decision? What is the moral decision?

The proposition is this . . .

This community would push the fat man to his death.

They vote. The result simply hangs in the air. Presumably fewer people have voted to push the man than the lever. In which case **Rob** *can say . . .*

It's different when you have to push a person, right?

Maybe morality has nothing to do with numbers or the greater good. It's just about what you can live with.

In the unlikely event that more people want to push the man than the lever **Rob** *says . . .*

You have no idea who that man was.

Scene Three

October 2015–March 2016.

Rob I'll be honest, vandalising the councillor's driveway had been childishly exhilarating.

I had felt guilty and when I got back to Glasgow I googled her and I'm happy to say it made me feel a lot better about what I had done. She did seem pretty awful. She was independent but really her Facebook page read very much like that of a UKIP candidate's. All union flags and Britain first and British jobs for British people. I had no idea that Scotland had these little pockets of bigots. I always thought we were better than England in that way.

Sorry.

I was just relieved to find that the target of my abuse had deserved it.

In October 2015 Cardiff University voted to no-platform Germain Greer for her anti-trans views and I actually cheered. Fuck her! She can have those views, we just don't want to hear them. And Eric agreed.

Between October 2015 and March 2016 I visited him three more times. Not to work on the script, just because he kept asking me and, well, I had time on my hands. I had handed in draft one of 'The Man Who Sold His Vote' to Ben and I was just waiting for the green light to start thinking about production dates and casting.

I was on a high.

Quite literally actually.

Now, I've never really smoked weed but up there, well, it seemed like the right thing to do.

With every trip Eric would tell me more and more about his years in political circles. More and more about the differences he had made in people's lives. The political party he had started in the eighties. The mining strikes he had attended in solidarity. The marches he'd been on, the pressure he had helped put on governments over the years. And it all started to make sense.

This was a man who for whatever reason had moved to this small town and found himself . . . A revolutionary in a town without need of a revolution.

So he had decided to invent one.

And a funny thing was happening to me. I was beginning, for the first time in my life, to feel politically motivated.

Why, I asked him one evening . . . in November I think it was . . . did you move here in the first place?

He looks at me for a long, long time. Finally seems to decide I've earned his trust.

Eric   I got in trouble. With the law. Went away for a while.

Rob   To prison?

Eric   No, to Antigua. Of course to prison.

Rob   What did you do?

Eric The party we set up. The Socialist Front. We went bust. Tried to make some money to keep it going. Ended up doing something stupid.

Rob What?

Eric Are you left wing Rob?

Rob What?

Eric Just answer. Yes or no.

Rob I wouldn't say I'm entirely . . .

Eric Yes or no.

Rob Yes. In that case. Yes.

Eric Are you pro-war?

Rob That's a difficult . . . what kind of war?

Eric Yes or no? Wars or not?

Rob No. No wars.

Eric Do you think violence is sometimes an acceptable means to a political end?

Yes or no.

Rob Yes?

Eric You don't sound sure.

Rob I'm not.

Eric Final question.

Have you stopped beating your wife?

Rob What? I never . . .

Eric Yes or no. Have you stopped beating your wife?

Rob I don't . . .

Eric Yes or fucking no?!

Rob   No. Technically that's the right answer. No.

Eric   So you still beat your wife . . .

Rob   I didn't . . .

But he's up and gone. Out into the night. Leaving me in his kitchen.

I watch as he goes down to the bottom of the garden and stands by the hives.

I go down and join him. Braving the possibility of a sting or two.

(And this is actually where I was stung for the first time but let's not dwell on that because it derails the flow.)

You okay?

Eric   Have you ever heard of the trolley problem, Rob?

Rob   No.

Eric   A runaway trolley is heading towards five railway workers.

Rob   A trolley?

Eric   A train car. It's just an old-fashioned . . . listen.

There is a runaway train car heading towards five railway workers. There's no time to warn them. They will die if it hits them. You are standing by a lever which, when pushed, will send the train car onto a siding on which there is a single workman. If you push the lever you will kill him but the five workers will be saved.

Do you push the lever?

Rob   Yeah. I think so.

Eric   Greater good, right?

Rob   Right.

Eric   Do you have a kid, Rob?

Rob   Not yet. We're trying.

Eric   What if it was your kid playing on the railway siding. And pushing the lever would kill him or her. Do you push it now?

Rob   No.

Eric   You let the five workers die don't you?

Rob   I do.

Eric   What happened to the greater good?

. . .

Rob   I didn't see Eric at all over Christmas. To be honest, after our weird night I thought our friendship might have run its course.

But then one day in March 2016 I get a message on Twitter.

Rob! It's happening. Immigrants are moving in all over the fucking place. Nazis have planned a big protest in Aberdeen. I'm organising a counter-protest. Please say you'll come with me. See what I'm all about. The real me.

Now, a bit of context.

Ben Power, the man with the greatest name in British theatre, had recently gotten back in touch to let me know they weren't going to go ahead with 'The Man Who Sold His Vote'. He thought the script was a little far from what we had originally discussed. He was still keen to do something with me but . . . what?

Maybe it was the desperation to find a story or maybe . . . I just wanted to go up there. I wanted to feel a part of something. To feel like I was making a difference. To demonstrate my social worth. To signal my virtue.

Whatever it was. It took me all of three minutes to agree to go to Aberdeen.

Scene Four

Present day.

Rob   There is a runaway train car heading towards five railway workers. There's no time to warn them. They will die if it hits them. You are standing by a lever which, when pushed, will send the train car onto a siding on which stands . . . your loved one. If you push the lever you will kill them but the five workers will be saved.

It's the same as before only this time I want you to picture the person you love more than anyone else in the world.

What is the correct decision? What is the moral decision?

The proposition is this . . .

This community would push the lever.

Rob *comments on the result. In all likelihood the number of people pushing the lever will be lower than ever.*

Okay. I hear you.

There is a runaway train car heading towards five non-violent Nazis (they hold the views without committing violence). There's no time to warn them. They will die if it hits them. You are standing by a lever which, when pushed, will send the train car onto a siding on which stands a normal left-wing/right-wing voter. If you push the lever you will kill the left-wing/right-wing voter but the five Nazis will be saved.

The proposition is this . . .

This community would push the lever (and save the Nazis).

Rob *comments on the result.*

I didn't know at the time but I have subsequently discovered that the White Hand are a non-violent organisation. Amongst their views, and I'm quoting from their website, they want to reintroduce Section 28, which prohibited the

the 'promotion of homosexuality' in schools and limit immigration of non-whites to zero. They are kind enough to say that any legal non-whites currently living here can stay. And they also emphasise their belief in a non-violent solution to this 'problem'.

They did have a base up near the town in which Eric was staying and there was a growing presence all along the north-east coast. So Eric was actually right about some of this.

This is one of their leaders. I follow him on Twitter. Ralph Weiss. He's Scottish but he changed his name. And as you can see he has an alarming number of followers.

This is his most recent tweet. He sent it this morning at 8.36 a.m.

We are sleepwalking to our demise. Immigration is killing Germany and it will kill us too. White lives matter.

Now. This morning I set up a Twitter account for this specific audience as I have done and will do for all audiences who see this show. Here it is. It's got today's date on it. It will exist for ever and its legacy will be one single tweet of defiance in the face of fascism. But only if you want to.

So. The proposition is . . .

This community wants to reply to Ralph Weiss.

Rob *comments on the result. If they don't want to reply the show moves on. If they do we move on to the next element.*

Okay. The majority has spoken. Now. We have two options for what to reply. But I'm not going to tell you what they are. I'm simply going to make the following proposition.

This community believes that people with abhorrent views deserve respect.

Please be honest. And vote now. Yes or No.

The audience vote. If they vote No then **Rob** *says . . .*

I thought you would say that. So we're going to ignore the polite reply which was . . .

That's fascinating. Why do you believe that?

Boring.

And go with this.

Fuck you, Ralph. Your kind of thinking is not welcome here. The people of this community wouldn't piss on you if you were on fire. Get cancer and die.

Much more what he deserves.

Rob *sends the message.*

However, if they vote Yes then **Rob** *says . . .*

Okay so we want to be polite. An interesting strategy. So let's ignore the nasty message, which was about his views not being welcome and wishing unpleasantness upon him and go with . . .

That's fascinating. Why do you believe that?

Rob *sends the message.*

There. I'm sure that will solve the Nazi problem once and for all. Hope you're happy with yourselves. The right-wing audiences have got more balls/even the left-wing audiences sent the nasty reply!

Either way, **Rob** *can sense the audience are not entirely happy with him.*

I can see some of you are upset. If you don't believe me that the system is legit you don't have to vote, you don't even have to stay, you can choose to disenfranchise yourself at any time if you are unsatisfied.

I mean, you chose this. This community agreed with how the show would run.

And anyway, don't worry. None of this is real. It's just theatre.

Scene Five

March 2016.

Rob March 2016 and I've become what I think is referred to as a keyboard warrior. I'm no longer scared of confrontation, no longer apathetic to politics, quite the opposite. Eric has . . . activated me.

I have at least half a dozen ongoing Twitter feuds going with dickheads of varying flavours. Anti-vaccination morons, right-wing racists, anti-immigration thugs, pro-life nutjobs and anti-feminist loons.

And I'm slaying them left, right and centre. Fuck you! You have no idea what you're talking about! You're abhorrent! Wrong side of history! Scum!

Eric is right, these people have got to be told, they've got to hear the noise of condemnation or they'll never change.

The ones I really hate are the ones who try to pretend to be reasonable. Who try to engage you in semantics or logical tricks. No. Fuck off. You don't support LGBTQ rights – that tells me all I need to know about you!

Fuck off!

I'm getting extremely excited about Aberdeen. My wife is a little upset that I've been taking so many trips up north but I explain to her I've got a play to write.

I arrive in Aberdeen train station and see Eric immediately. But he doesn't look happy. There's something missing there.

Eric The Nazis salted the hives.

Rob What?

Eric The bees have gone. The majority. I think someone salted them out.

Rob I'm sorry.

Eric Don't get sorry, get even.

Rob   He says.

Eric   Let's go.

Rob   We head up to the high street and at first it seems like any other city on a Saturday afternoon. But then . . . slowly they emerge. The protestors. Looking exactly like you or me, but . . . different somehow. Hardened. Stern. No room for fun in their lives. Not until they've fixed this problem.

As we get closer to the high street the regular people begin to become outnumbered and as we turn the last corner I see it . . . the protest.

Eric   Fuck me.

Rob   Says Eric.

Eric   More than I thought.

Rob   It is alarming how many people have shown up to protest against the arrival of desperate immigrants from a war-torn country. But heartening to see that the counter-protest still outnumbers them around two to one.

Eric has made a beeline to the front line. I remember thinking as he arrived and shook hands: None of these people recognise him. He said he'd organised this.

We stood there, looking across the main road, through the traffic, at the enemy on the other side. Placards hoisted high.

'BRITAIN FIRST'. 'WHITE MIGHT'. 'KEEP SCOTLAND SAFE'.

They can't all be Nazis, I say to Eric.

Eric   No. Some of them will be plain old right-wing bigots.

Rob   And before I know it Eric is screaming at the top of his lungs . . .

If you're right, you're wrong. If you're right, you're wrong. If you're right, you're wrong!

And our side are joining in. And I join in. It's my first political chant. I'm giddy.

The opposition retort with a chorus of 'SCOTLAND FIRST', 'SCOTLAND FIRST', but we hit back at them with . . .

'FUCK OFF, BIGOTS, FUCK OFF!'

It's not clever but it's to the point.

There is rage in the air but I've never felt safer. I can't explain it, I just thought . . . This is where I'm meant to be. Doing something. Standing up for something. Shouting about something. At this time on a Saturday I'm usually in my underwear watching football on TV. But now I'm out here standing up for immigrants. It felt great.

Eric *spots a group of protestors whom he seems to recognise.*

Eric   That's them! That's the White Hand guys.

'NAZI SCUM, NAZI SCUM!'

Rob   He screams over and over again at them. So loud that some of the police who are surrounding the protestors actually turn and look over the road towards us.

This is great isn't it? I say to Eric.

Eric   It's pathetic. Standing here on two sides of a road. They've not even bothered to stop traffic. And they know what they're doing. Just standing there. With their signs. Those signs are incitement to hatred. Those signs are violent. And the police just stand there. They know as long as they don't do anything we can't raise a finger against them.

Rob   Would we want to?

Eric   Words are never going to change their minds.

Rob   He's probably right, I think.

Eric   I mean if you can't punch a Nazi who can you punch?

Rob   And so the day goes on. Three hours we stand there, taking breaks to head to the pub for pints and snacks. Coming back and chanting some more. Getting to know the anti-protestors. A nice bunch. Normal people concerned with stopping fascism.

By five o'clock Eric and I are pissed and the protest across the road is winding down.

And I can tell Eric is disappointed.

And to be honest, I am too. We just let them stand there all day spewing ignorance and hate. They'll be leaving now thinking they've won. Fuck.

The day has been a failure.

And as we're walking back to the station . . .

As dusk is settling in over the granite city . . .

We come upon a lone protestor.

Eric   He's one of the White Hand.

Rob   Whispers Eric.

Rob   He's holding a sign that reads, 'NO MORE IMMIGRANTS'.

He's on his phone and he's . . . laughing.

And joking.

He thinks his side have won the argument. But he can't have won because there were more of us! Why does he think he's won?!

And something inside me snaps.

A combination of rage, excitement, alcohol and . . . finally understanding why it's important to care . . .

Because it's not fake. It's not theatre. It's right here. It's real and it's in front of me.

I pick up my pace . . .

I position myself behind this guy . . .

And I just . . .

Swing.

From behind.

With my fist clenched.

And I punch him on the side of the head.

And it doesn't hurt.

And I catch him sweet.

And he drops to the ground.

And his phone smashes on the cobbled street.

. . .

. . .

Two policemen nearby have seen the whole thing.

I didn't even bother to check . . .

I was on autopilot.

And as I turned around, my hands held out before me, welcoming the arrest, I remember thinking . . .

Worth it.

I did the right thing.

But as they arrest me I realise . . .

Eric has run away.

. . .

In the morning, when I had sobered up and I realised I was going to be prosecuted – I pled guilty and received a six-month suspended sentence – I didn't feel quite so good about myself.

The guy, as I found out in court, wasn't a member of the White Hand. He worked for a charity that housed the homeless of Scotland and was bitterly disappointed with the housing going to Syrians rather than homeless Scots. A reasonable position I suppose.

I reached out to him but he understandably didn't want anything to do with me.

I decided likewise to cut ties with Eric. Completely.

A letter arrived a few weeks later in his handwriting. I couldn't bring myself to throw it in the bin but I also didn't want to open it and risk being sucked back in to that world. I put it in a drawer. I'll open it when it's safe.

I was thoroughly ashamed of myself. And I just wanted to forget all about Eric and everything that had happened.

Safer not caring about things, I remember thinking.

Act Three

A domestic scene. **Rob** *is home again.*

Scene One

Present day.

Rob   Now, I've noticed some of you squirming in the seats, which suggests there may be more than a few of you that require a toilet break. But I'll tell you now, we are building up a head of steam so to break now would not be wise.

But this is a democracy so let's find out if people want to have mercy on the people who are in pain – because it is painful, isn't it, needing to wee.

So, the proposition is this . . .

This community believes that we should derail the show so the minority can be more comfortable.

Please vote now.

If the result is Yes, **Rob** *stops the show and allows the minority to go to the toilet. Ideally, and more likely, the audience will vote No, in which case* **Rob** *simply continues the show.*

At one point, after I decided it couldn't be about Eric, I thought my show was going to be about the dangers of referendums. How the minority suffer under the tyranny of the majority. But then David Cameron went and made that show for real.

I voted.

In the Brexit referendum.

My first time ever.

It was okay. Quite exciting really. But I chose the wrong answer. So it didn't really do much for my confidence in the system.

Do you ever wish you could turn back time? Change a decision that you had made?

What did this community vote in that referendum? Do you mind me asking?

Why don't we do a rerun.

The proposition is . . .

This community believed that the UK should remain in the EU.

Please vote as you did back then.

They vote.

So there are a lot of unhappy/happy people in this room.

They say if they ran the vote again we would find that a lot of people who voted No would vote Yes.

. . .

But it doesn't work that way does it?

If only we could go back. Shout louder. Call more Brexiteers racist. Call more of them idiots. Maybe even punch a few of them. The result might have been different.

Scene Two

June 2016.

Rob   June 2016. The UK is in shock. Again. Brexit has triumphed. The majority have spoken.

If this was 2014 I wouldn't feel so bad about this.

I log onto Facebook. I've not been on in months. I check my messages. It's mainly my liberal friends, who've heard what happened to me, praising my choice to punch the man for what he thought.

I delete my account. Quickly, before I have the chance to reconsider.

A message tells me it will be there for a month if I reconsider.

I do the same with my Twitter account.

Better fingers in the ears than a fist in the face.

My wife chooses this day to tell me she's pregnant. My first thought is, shit. What have we done? What world is this child going to inherit? How can I teach him how to live when I've no idea myself?

I need to speak to Eric. I don't know why, but I do. I just do.

But I've deleted my account. And there's no way I'm reactivating it so soon. So instead I pick up my mobile and call his landline number.

It rings and rings and finally Lucy picks up.

Oh. Hello. It's Rob. I was looking for Eric.

Lucy Oh fuck.

Rob She says.

Lucy You haven't heard.

Rob What?

Lucy Rob. Eric is dead.

Scene Three

July–November 2016.

Rob Between July and November of 2016 I visit Lucy three times.

Here's what I found out on the first visit.

Eric came home after Aberdeen deeply depressed.

They didn't see much of him for a while.

And then one day she came round to the house to drop off
Morag and . . . he was gone.

There was no note. And all of his things were still there. But
she knew something was wrong because there were bees, the
ones who hadn't left, buzzing and dying all over the kitchen.

She called the police. They said there's not much they could
do. He's a grown man. He decided to leave.

Lucy insisted he would never just leave. He must have
thrown himself into the sea or something. Or . . . maybe
the Nazis had killed him. He was always saying they would
one day.

They said they'd keep an eye out for him. But there was no
evidence of any crime.

But there was. Or so Lucy thought. Because on the kitchen
table was a little porcelain figure of a woman holding a flame
above her head. Kind of like the statue of liberty but . . . not.
It didn't belong to Eric. He would never buy such a thing.
He hated tat like that.

It had to mean something.

'What?' the police asked her.

But she couldn't tell them.

By the second visit she had sold his house. She needed the
money. We sat in her living room with Morag colouring in in
the corner.

Lucy   It's called the Goddess of Liberty. The statue. It
could have been a message. About freedom of speech or
something. From the Nazis.

Rob   Maybe he just decided he needed some time away.

Lucy   Why would he do that to us?

Rob   He might have thought you were better off
without him.

Lucy   Do you think that Rob?

Rob   What? No. No I don't.

Lucy   None of this feels real.

Rob   The house smelled vaguely of weed. I watched Morag colour in. She was good at keeping in the lines.

By the third visit Lucy had given up. It was November and Donald Trump, the host of the *The Apprentice USA*, had become the President of the United States of America.

I imagined Eric, wherever he was, hearing about that. I told you so, Rob. I fucking told you so.

Lucy must have been the only person on the planet who hadn't heard.

Lucy   What did you say?

Rob   I said Trump won.

Lucy *laughs*.

Lucy   That's funny.

Rob   Lucy I'm going to stop coming up here. Is that okay?

Lucy   Why wouldn't it be?

Rob   No reason.

You know, Lucy, I've suffered from depression too.

Lucy   You don't say.

Rob   And withdrawing isn't really the answer.

Lucy   Says you.

Rob   Yeah. Says me.

Lucy   So what's the answer?

Rob   Well . . . I tried being like Eric.

Lucy   Ha. That was your first mistake.

Rob   So now . . . I don't really know what to do. I know I
care. I'm glad about that. I know I want to do something.
It's just . . .

How do you care without hurting?

Lucy   If I knew that, Rob, I wouldn't be sitting here with
the likes of fucking you, would I?

Scene Four

February 2017.

Rob   February of 2017. I'm in my new house in
Loughborough – my wife got a job – and I'm reading an
article online that's made my blood run cold.

In America, a neo-Nazi by the name of Richard Spencer was
punched in the face by a protester during a live TV
interview.

And the *Guardian* published an article that said . . .

'A punch may be uncivil, but racism is worse. When
criticising tactics against racism, it's important to prioritise.'

A national liberal newspaper published an article that
defended punching people for holding opinions.

But instead of feeling vindicated in my own actions,
I felt sick.

I see a link on the sidebar about a Facebook post. My
account has long gone so I'm eager to see it.

It's a post from a Hillary Clinton supporter suggesting it
might be a good thing if Trump was assassinated.
Underneath someone has linked to a post from a Klu Klux
Klan member from 2008 who had said the exact same thing
about Obama.

Another hyperlink takes me to this quote from a Trump
supporter.

'They all said I'd be racist to vote for Trump. They made lists of words I wasn't allowed to say. They said, hey white people, stop being racist. Which has got to be the single most ironic sentence ever written. And you know what? That just made me want to vote for him all the more. Don't tell me what I am. Don't tell me how to think. Fuck you for doing that. This is on you, not me.'

Now, I'll admit that actually I read these things months apart, but the story is neater if it was one long hyperlink journey.

I close the laptop as my mum enters the room holding her grandson.

Mum   Yes, yes you are, yes you are. Yes. Yes you are.

Rob   My son is something that much is clear. I'm just not sure what.

Mum   You are the cutest little boy. Yes you are.

Rob   Ah. Right. That clears that up.

Mum   You know if I was American I think I'd have voted for Trump too. I mean it's funny, isn't it. It's like a TV show, you want to see what happens next!

Rob   My baby boy stares at me. He's not smiling yet. Just looking. Checking shit out. Deciding whether or not this whole being born thing has been a good idea or not. He's on the fence so far. I can tell.

Mum   He is the cutest little boy. Isn't he? Yes you are. Yes you are, Eric. Yes you are.

Oh, by the way, I was unpacking boxes and I found this. You've not opened it.

Rob   And she hands me the letter.

How could I have forgotten about the fucking letter?!

The letter Eric had sent me one week before he had disappeared.

Scene Four

Present day.

Rob *holds the letter in his hand.*

Rob   Let's just see if we've got a reply from our tweet earlier.

Yes. He's usually replied by this point in the show.

Here we go.

Rob *reads out the reply. It's either . . .*

'I told you last night I don't give a fuck what a theatre audience thinks – stop messaging, losers!'

Or . . .

'I'd be happy to talk about anything you like. Please DM me and we can arrange a time and place.'

Rob *comments briefly on this reply. Then turns his attention to the letter in his hand.*

This isn't the real letter. Well it is. Kind of. It's a replica. A prop. But it is real. Because the words are exactly the same.

This letter is the key to everything. To Eric's disappearance. The significance of the porcelain figure. The truth about his past.

But I'm afraid we have a problem.

Because also in this letter are explicit instructions from Eric that what is contained within this letter never be divulged to anyone.

This is all true. It's what I've built the show around. When I got this letter I knew how the show would end. Which any writer will tell you is the key to the whole enterprise. And I also knew that it was too perfect. You would never believe me.

But it's true. Eric, wherever he is, dead or alive, genuinely does not want this to be publicly known. This was for me only.

So I'm faced with a conundrum. Because the contents of this letter are undoubtedly valuable. To me. To you. To society. To our present sense of fulfilment and to our future happiness as we dissolve this small community and head back into our wider one. The community would benefit but Eric and those he loves, Lucy and Morag, would suffer.

I'd like you all to vote now not to hear this. To ruin your own experience. To make that sacrifice to honour the wishes of someone who is not here to defend himself.

So . . .

The proposition is this.

This community believes this letter should remain unread.

Please vote now.

The audience vote.

If the result is Yes, **Rob** *thanks them and skips straight to the epilogue.*

It the result is No, Rob reads the letter.

It's long but I'm going to read all of it.

Dear Rob.

I'm sorry. That's the first thing I need to say to you. I left you there and it haunts me. Fucking haunts me, man.

I need to explain. You know I've been in jail and so does Lucy. I told her it was for fraud but that's not true. In 1984 when we were trying to raise funds to start our party and get a deposit together to run for parliament we did something really fucking stupid. We robbed a bank. Banks were smaller back then. It's not as flash as it sounds. Our guns weren't even loaded. Anyway the idea was not to hurt anyone, just get in and take some money, enough to get us going and no one would be hurt. In fact, the community would benefit because our party was exactly what was needed. It was for the greater good, we thought. I still do. But during the robbery a security guard decided to be a hero and I clocked him over the head with the end of my gun. And he fucking died, didn't he? Anyway, that's why I was in jail and I've never told Lucy that because I don't want Morag knowing her dad's a fucking murderer. Part of the conditions of my early release were that if I was caught in any situations like the one we found ourselves in I'd go straight back inside, no questions asked.

I couldn't punch the fucker so I put you in that position. And I'm sorry.

My whole life has been about making a difference and I've done fuck all. Do you ever hate the sound of your own voice? In the middle of talking I'm thinking, I hate myself but I can't stop it. I know I'm not helping but I get so angry at the world that I can't stop raging.

Because I know you care, Rob. Despite what you say. Your nihilism's a defence mechanism. Like Lucy's pretending nothing's real. If I don't care about anything then nothing can hurt me. That's you, Rob. That's what you pretend to be. A sociopath. When really you're one of the most caring people I've ever met.

Anyway, I'm done, Rob. I'm out. I'm leaving and I'm not coming back. But I've left you a present on the table in the kitchen. You asked me once if we'd ever all agree and get along. Well the answer's no. And that's a good thing, mate. Agreement is anathema to progress. Remember that. Never stop caring, never stop disagreeing. Just find a better way to do it. Be better than me.

You can tell Lucy I'm not coming back but please, please don't tell her anything else that's in this letter. Any of it. Don't tell anyone.

I know you'll do that for me.

With love, comrade.

Eric.

Epilogue

June 2017.

Rob   June 2017, I'm back in the office of Professor Duncan. Because I know every good story needs bookending.

The Labour Party has performed better than expected leaving the country with a hung parliament.

Fuck. We might actually have to talk to each other.

He asks me how I voted and I tell him . . . Greens.

Duncan   I respect that, son, I respect that.

Rob   It's actually only the second time I've ever voted, I admit.

Duncan   So you didn't vote in the indy referendum after all?

Rob   No.

Duncan   Well. Make sure you vote in the next one.

Rob   You're not angry?

Duncan   Why would I be angry?

Rob   Last time I was here . . .

Duncan   Yes, I've felt bad about that since you left the office. I was in a piss poor mood. I should have been more civil. Tell me, did you ever go visit that guy who sold his vote?

Rob   I did.

Duncan   And how did it go?

Rob　I tell him I got in trouble. I punched some guy.

Duncan　Why?

Rob　Because he didn't . . . He was . . . He had a really bad opinion . . .

He looks at me and says . . .

Duncan　The rules one puts in place, the principles and laws by which a community lives should be exactly the same principles as one would like to be in place when the people we disagree with are in power.

Rob　What does that mean?

Duncan　It means that some people might think your views are equally punch-worthy.

Pause.

Rob　I decide to take a chance.

Greg.

How do you care without hurting?

He stares at me.

What I mean is . . .

Duncan　I know what you mean, I'm just thinking.

Rob　He thinks for a full minute. Then says . . .

Duncan　How does it feel to be wrong, Rob?

Rob　Eh. Not good. You feel silly.

Duncan　No. That's how it feels to find out you're wrong.

Rob　Oh.

Duncan　How does it feel to be wrong?

Rob　It feels . . . exactly the same as being right.

Duncan　Exactly.